Designer Fabrics of the Early '60s

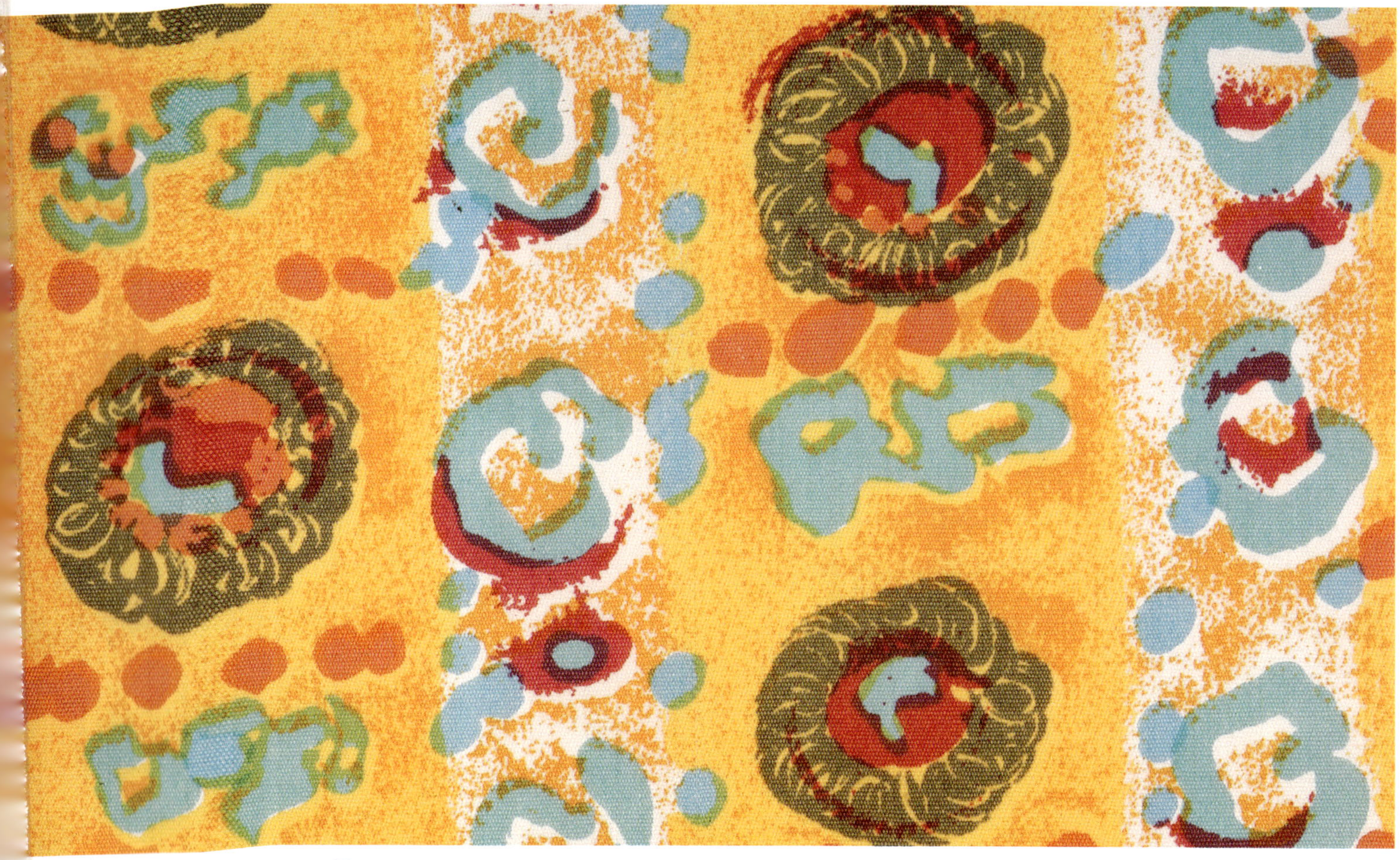

Tina Skinner

4880 Lower Valley Road, Atglen, PA 19310

Copyright © 1998 by Schiffer Publishing Ltd.
Library of Congress Catalog Card Number: 97-80677

All rights reserved. No part of this work may be reproduced or used in any form or by any means—graphic, electronic, or mechanical, including photocopying or information storage and retrieval systems—without written permission from the copyright holder.

Book design by Blair R. Loughrey

ISBN: 0-7643-0506-9
Printed in Hong Kong

Published by Schiffer Publishing Ltd.
4880 Lower Valley Road
Atglen, PA 19310
Phone: (610) 593-1777; Fax: (610) 593-2002
E-mail: SchifferBk@aol.com
Please write for a free catalog.
This book may be purchased from the publisher.
Please include $3.95 for shipping.

Try your bookstore first.

We are interested in hearing from authors with book ideas on related subjects.

Contents

Introduction 4

Florals 6

Plaids, Stripes, and Other "Orderly" Patterns 33

Abstracts 64

Black and White 80

Novelty 87

Upholstery and Home-decorating Fabrics 97

Bibliography 112

Introduction

The biggest fashion icon of the early 1960s was Jacqueline Kennedy, who struck a pose at the turn of the decade as her husband campaigned for, and won, the presidency, in 1961. The woman everyone wanted to mirror, Kennedy was rarely seen in anything other than solids, a fact that didn't bode well for the print designers of her day. This was further compounded by fashions that dictated wasp-thin waists and thighs, a look best obtained with solids or, at most, vertical stripes.

The austerity of World War II still seemed all too recent as its hero, Dwight D. Eisenhower, finished up his second term as president in 1961, and the styles people wore reflected this self-conscious, conservative tone. The colors of the era were not very adventurous. Nature's warm shades were in, bearing monikers like beige, stone green, olive green, ivory, lilac, sea blue, royal blue, gold, and brass, with the boldest of the bunch being burnt orange, turquoise, mint, and lilac. By the end of John F. Kennedy's short reign, brighter hues were finally emerging—lemon, lime, orange, and aqua being the stars—though conservative greens, gold, beige, and black still held sway. The styles were equally conservative, with a spattering of plaids and stripes, and the ever-popular floral prints.

Still, the couture fabric design houses in Paris were looking to the future. In this sampling of fabric designs from 1960-1963, we get glimpses of the hot colors that wouldn't make their way into small town America for another half decade, and we see the emergence of mod and continuing experi-

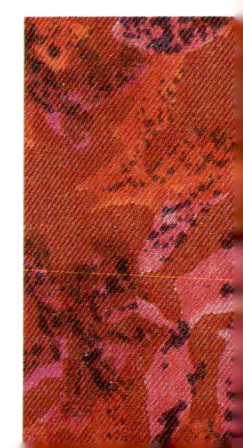

mentation with abstract designs. Orderly patterns like plaids, polka dots, and stripes were given new twists, and increasing technology in man-made fibers fostered experimentation, especially with home-decorating and other heavy, special-use fabrics.

This book includes a special section on Upholstery and Home-decorating Fabrics, as well as Florals, Plaids and Other "Orderly" Patterns, Abstracts, Black and White, and Novelty prints. It is an inspiring collection of more than 250 printed and woven designs. The full-color photos are from fabric swatch books published by designer textile manufacturers in Paris. Because the swatches are small, many don't show complete repeats. The year of publication is listed with each fabric sample, as well as fabric content, if known. The word "blend" indicates an incomplete accounting of fabric content.

Small though they are, these swatches lend insight into one of art's higher forms, where painterly techniques were combined with mathematical precision to create repeating patterns for endless yards of fabric. Often overlooked, these works of art are paraded daily through malls and office buildings, factories and restaurants, on the backs and backsides of billions of people. Here, in small, beautifully detailed shots, we take a close look at the cream of the early 1960s crop from Paris's best couture houses. It is hoped that this book will instill in the reader an appreciation for this art form, and inspire others to emulate these master works.

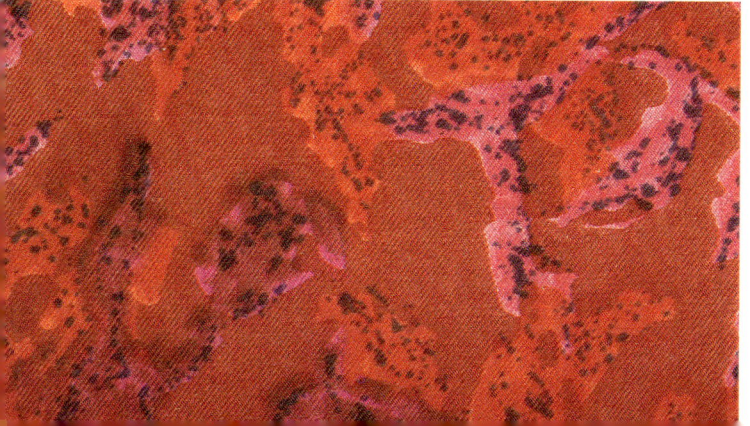

Florals

Light, all-over garden scene of flowers and foliage. Cotton crêpe de chine. 1961.

Watercolor effect in rich tones. Cotton/polyester. 1961.

Left:
Two-directional floral design. Cotton. 1960.

Below left:
The neutral colors in this abstract floral pattern are stung with sky blue highlights. Cotton. 1961.

Below right:
All-over floral silhouettes in blue and charcoal. Polyester blend. 1961.

Abstract, all-over water lily scene. Polyester blend. 1961.

Abstract garden motif in red, green, and blue. Cotton/polyester knit. 1961.

Green floral pattern on white ground. Cotton blend. 1960.

Stylized floral motif on gold ground. Silk. 1963.

Radiating flower design in five shades of brown and beige. Polyester blend. 1961.

Childlike rendering of flowers and leafy vines, with fascinating, erratic outline effect. Silk. 1963.

Small, childlike flowers of lime with brass highlights leap off black ground. Rayon. 1961.

Above & Left:
Black and brown stylized floral design on polyester-blend knit has a much different look than the same pattern with brighter colors and mottled ground on cotton blend. 1961.

11

Above:
Traditional rose bouquets form a two-directional pattern on heavy fabric. Cotton/viscose blend. 1961.

Left:
Muted colors spilling beyond outlines create an out-of-focus effect for this floral scene. Silk blend. 1961.

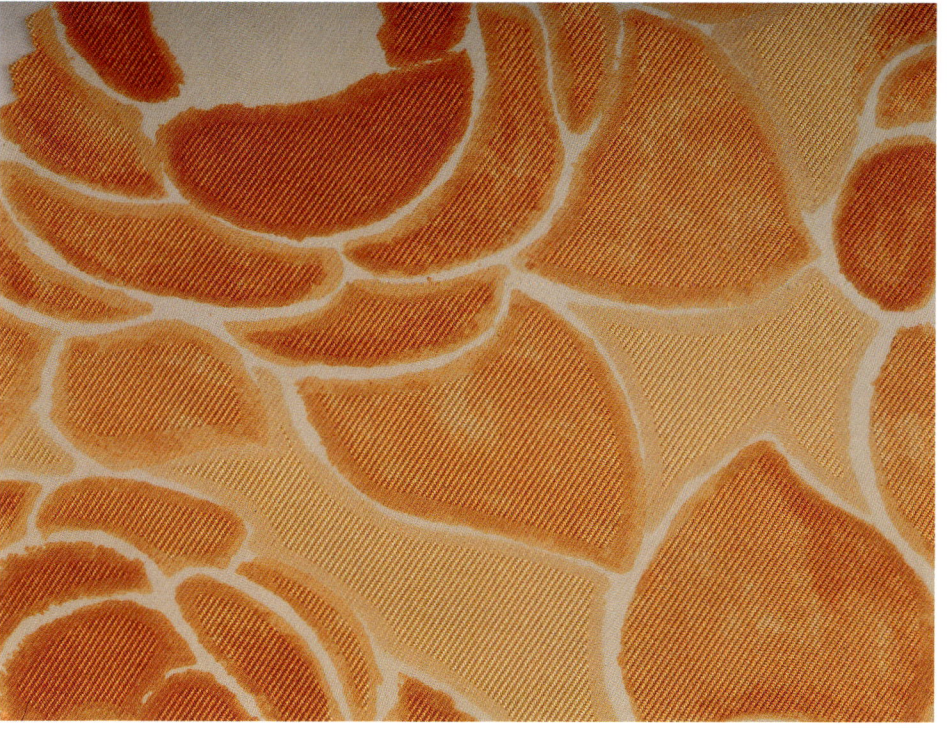

Above left:
Orange rose motif in stained-glass style with white leading. Silk. 1963.

Above right:
Simplistic, painted flowers of orange, lemon, and apricot with natural-tone leaves and ground. Silk. 1963.

Left:
Boldly outlined flowers stand out against abstract floral motif. Cotton. 1960.

Left:
Lollipop trees on beige ground. Rayon twill. 1963.

Lower left:
Cocoon flowers and their shadows form dotted grid. Polyester. 1963.

Lower right:
Childlike center circles and simplistic, outlined patches of petal color form polka-dot pattern. Cotton. 1960.

Left:
Flower garden rendered with childlike simplicity. Rayon. 1961.

Below left:
Pinks, oranges, and olive green create all-over floral pattern. Silk. 1963.

Below right:
Bold pink chrysanthemums on white ground. Rayon-blend twill. 1961.

Above left:
Bright florals on white ground. Polished cotton. 1963.

Above right:
1960. Blue, berry-like flowers punctuated by red cousins are grouped in garden motif. Cotton novelty weave.

Left:
Stylized rose pattern in blues and black. Polyester. 1963.

Above left:
Dotted ground with outline flowers and pink highlights. Polyester/cotton. 1960.

Above right:
Stylized, pink snowflake flowers on white ground. Cotton/polyester. 1963.

Left:
Floral design printed only on raised cords of novelty print. Cotton. 1960.

Above:
Blocks of color and tenuous outlines form abstract floral pattern. Cotton. 1960.

Above right:
Lollipop flowers adorn broad blue, green, and white stripes. Cotton. 1960.

Right:
Impressionistic roses float in all-over print. Nylon blend. 1961.

Radiating pinks create floral grid punctuated by green leaves. Cotton/polyester blend. 1960.

Large fuchsia, blue, and gold buds pack a white ground. Cotton/rayon. 1961.

Above:
Bold hatch pattern in charcoal with red and peach overlay leaving white, abstract flowers. Cotton. 1963.

Above right:
Red, pink, and gold are blended for this floral motif. Rayon blend. 1963.

Right:
Large rose motif with red leaves, printed on bird's-eye weave. Cotton. 1960.

Flowered lines, wash colors, and picotage evoke image of tie-dye. Cotton blend. 1963.

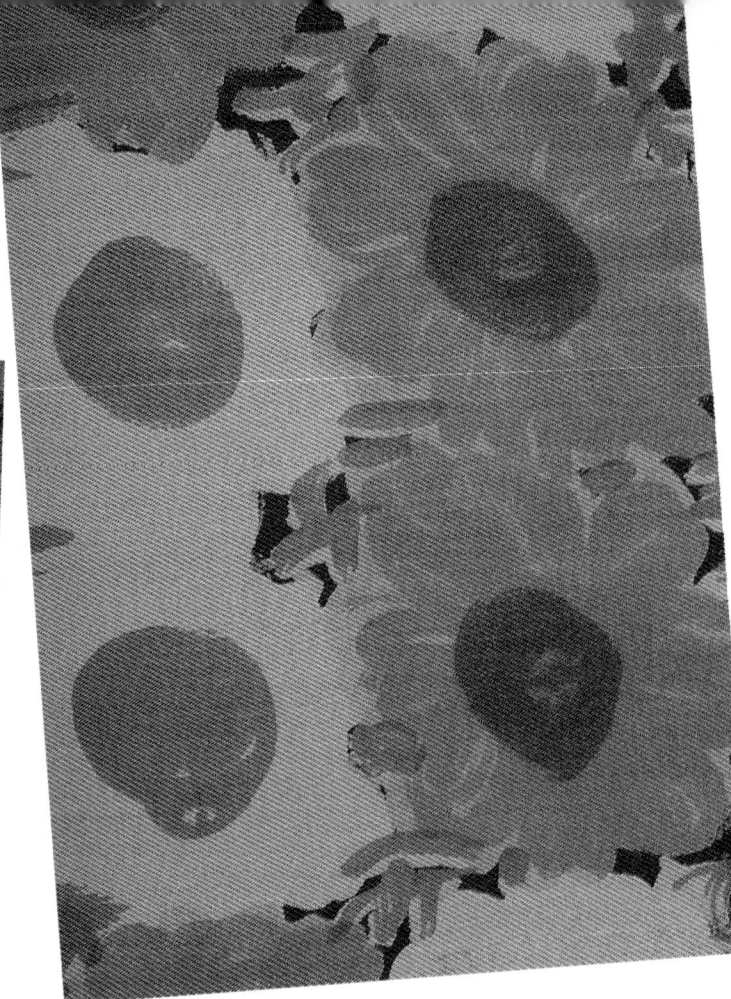

22

Above:
Painterly flower garden in natural tones. Rayon. 1961.

Above right:
Soft yellow and gray blooms arranged four-by-four create a floral plaid. Rayon. 1961.

Right:
Floral watercolor on yellow ground. Silk. 1963.

Above left:
Large, painterly pink blossoms contrast with bone ground. Cotton. 1960.

Above right:
Abstract roses on stormy, dark ground. Cotton/polyester. 1961.

Left:
Two-directional, bright floral print. Cotton crêpe. 1961.

Painterly rosebud pattern with distinctive, royal-blue outline. Nylon. 1961.

Blue and green floral motif on white ground. Cotton. 1960.

Colorful floral pattern. Cotton/polyester. 1960.

Jagged edges and black ground lend drama to classic rose design. Cotton twill. 1961.

Bright bouquets on tiger-stripe-yellow and flower-speckled ground. Cotton. 1963.

Peasant scenes and flower sprays in one-directional print. Polyester knit. 1961.

Bold floral sprays leap from mottled, muted-gray ground. Silk. 1961.

Contrasting colors are used to create image of broad brushstrokes for all-over floral image. Cotton blend. 1960.

Bold floral design with white highlights. Cotton/polyester blend. 1960.

Painterly gold roses with spindly stems and black leaves against packed blue rose and swirls ground. Rayon. 1960.

Dark tulips are created with bold brushstrokes. Rayon/polyester. 1961.

Roses emerge from violent crosshatches of dark colors. Silk. 1961.

Rich colors gild this impressionistic flower garden. Cotton/rayon. 1961.

Above:
Floral brocade dominated by black plastic threads. Cotton blend. 1963.

Above right & right:
Same pattern of metallic gold-thread embroidery over two very different prints. Rayon blend. 1963.

Above: Persian block print pattern with floral motif. Polyester blend. 1961.

Left: Ornate plaid packed with flowers and leaves. Rayon blend. 1961.

Black outlines predominate this print, giving it a wrought-iron appearance. Note the early mod-style flowers. Polyester blend. 1961.

Abstract floral mosaic is created from natural tones. Silk. 1961.

Above:
Floral motif punctuates diagonal, zigzag stripes. Cotton/polyester. 1961.

Right:
Painterly, flower-filled plaid of blues. Cotton. 1961.

Left:
Diagonal plaid created in Southwestern colors—rust, turquoise, black, and gold, on olive ground. Viscose/wool. 1960.

Below:
Black lines on red ground imitate open weave. Cotton. 1963.

Plaids, Stripes, and Other "Orderly" Patterns

Above:
Grid pattern. Rayon. 1963.

Above right:
Red diagonal stripes of branch or antler shapes form harlequin pattern. Wool. 1963.

Right:
Circles and diamonds form large harlequin pattern. Cotton. 1963.

Green, brown, and pink squares on white ground. Cotton novelty weave. 1960.

Abstract plaid of small blocks of color. Rayon. 1961.

Camouflage colors are used in this plaid design with shocking white highlights. Polyester/cotton. 1961.

Above:
Olive green plaid with dark green, dotted stripes. Nylon. 1960.

Above right:
Loose harlequin design shimmers with metallic vertical threads. Rayon blend. 1961.

Right:
Three-directional stripes form grid pattern. Rayon. 1963.

Above:
Geometric foliage and crosshatching are used for patchwork effect. Thick cotton weave. 1960.

Left:
Jumbled hound's-tooth design. Cotton/polyester. 1961.

Opposite:
Metallic and black-plastic threads emerge in squares over mottled ground. Rayon blend. 1963.

Above:
Patchwork plaid design. Cotton. 1961.

Right:
Stacked empty and circle-filled squares create a plaid pattern. Viscose, rayon blend. 1961.

Above:
Abstract blue and green plaid on cotton velvet. 1960.

Above right:
Packed paisley plaid. Cotton. 1960.

Right:
Tromp l'oeil geometric design. Silk. 1963.

Above:
Soft, geometric grid with white snowflakes and winter-blue tones. Silk. 1963.

Left:
Two-tone, blue, geometric foliage pattern. Cotton. 1963.

Above left:
Stylized and ornamented teardrop shapes create abstract winter pattern. Rayon blend. 1961.

Above:
Abstract design imitates basket weave. Rayon blend. 1961.

Left:
Blue and white, Dutch-motif design. Polyester. 1960.

Above right:
Gear-shaped patterns on black ground. Cotton. 1963.

Above:
Abstract geometric patterns punctuated by electric blue highlights. Cotton/rayon. 1961.

Right:
Abstract flowers and dots form colorful plaid. Rayon. 1963.

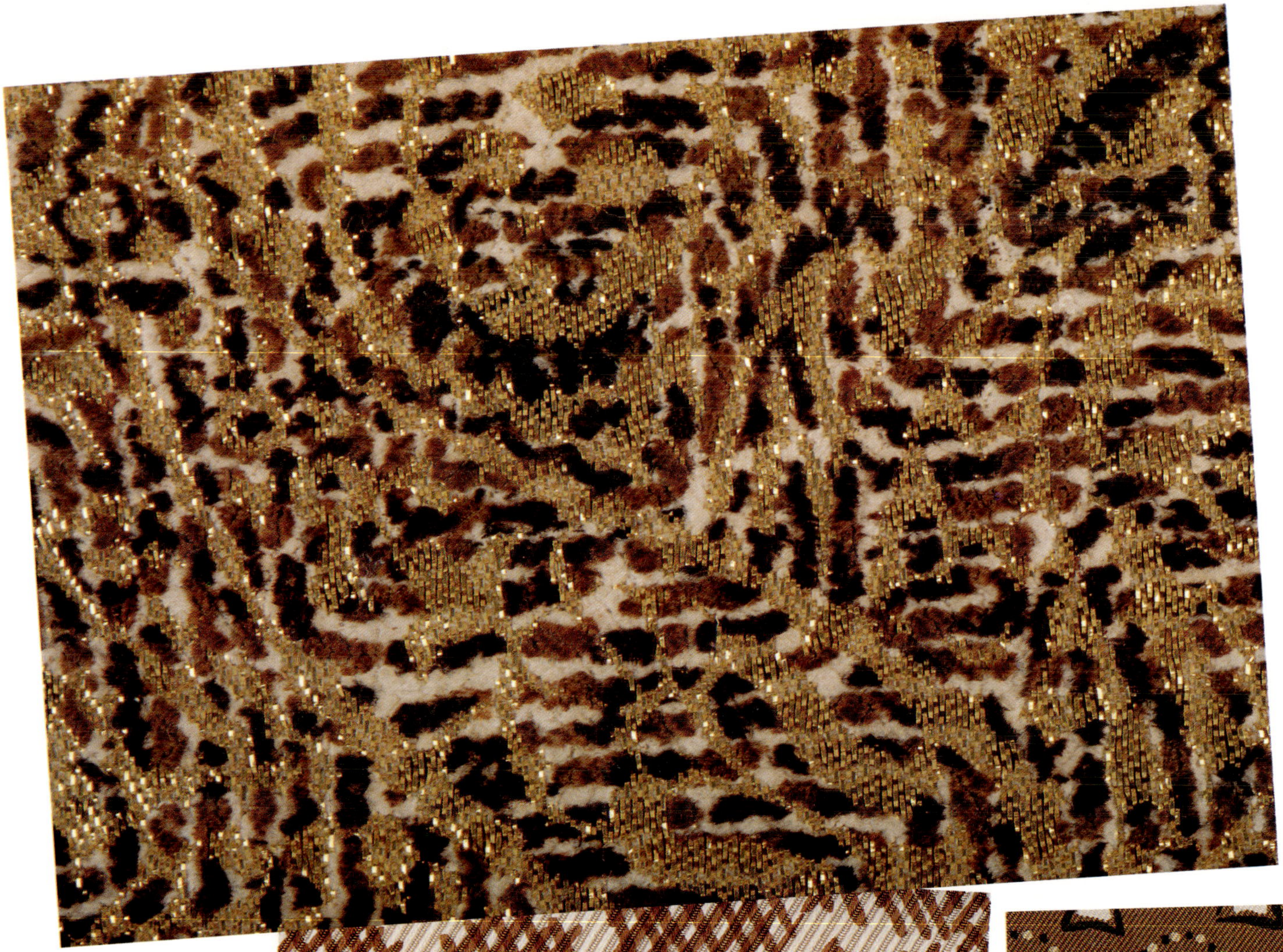

Left:
Square pattern of short, dark and light lines, overlaid by irregular metallic stripes. Nylon blend. 1961.

Below left:
Hatched dots. Rayon twill. 1963.

Below:
Simple, geometric design of squares and ringed circles. Rayon twill. 1961.

Cobblestone effect created by outlined blocks of color. Rayon blend. 1961.

Soft foulard design with offset metallic highlights. Silk blend. 1961.

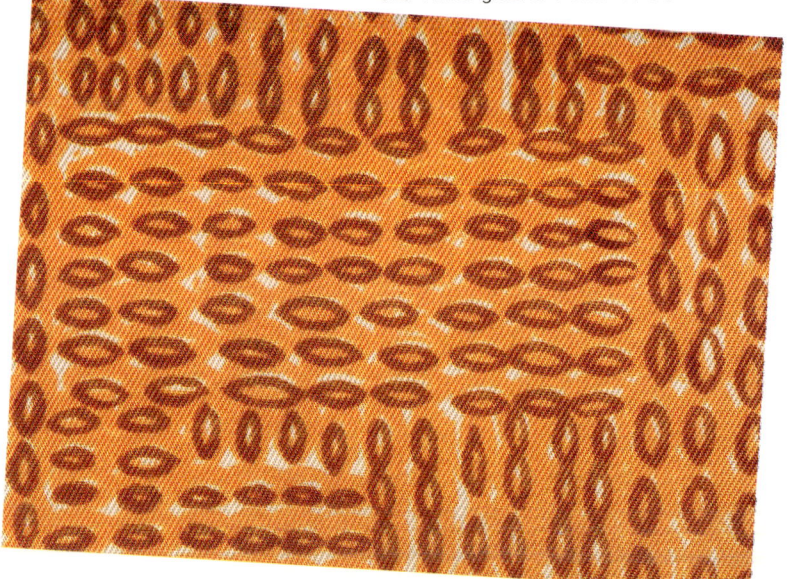

Brown ovals form patchwork over orange and white ground. Silk. 1963.

Greens and golds in swirling, zigzag design. Polished cotton. 1963.

Floral-motif stripes on unusual, polished burlap. 1960.

Above:
Green and gold floral motifs form stripes on white ground. Cotton. 1960.

Left:
Looped lines form a wickerwork plaid. Rayon blend. 1961.

Above:
Watercolor stripes in rough herringbone pattern temper bright pink ground. Rayon/polyester twill. 1961.

Above right:
Stripe design evokes wrought-iron fence image. Rayon. 1963.

Right:
Irregular green stripes create foliage effect. Rayon. 1961.

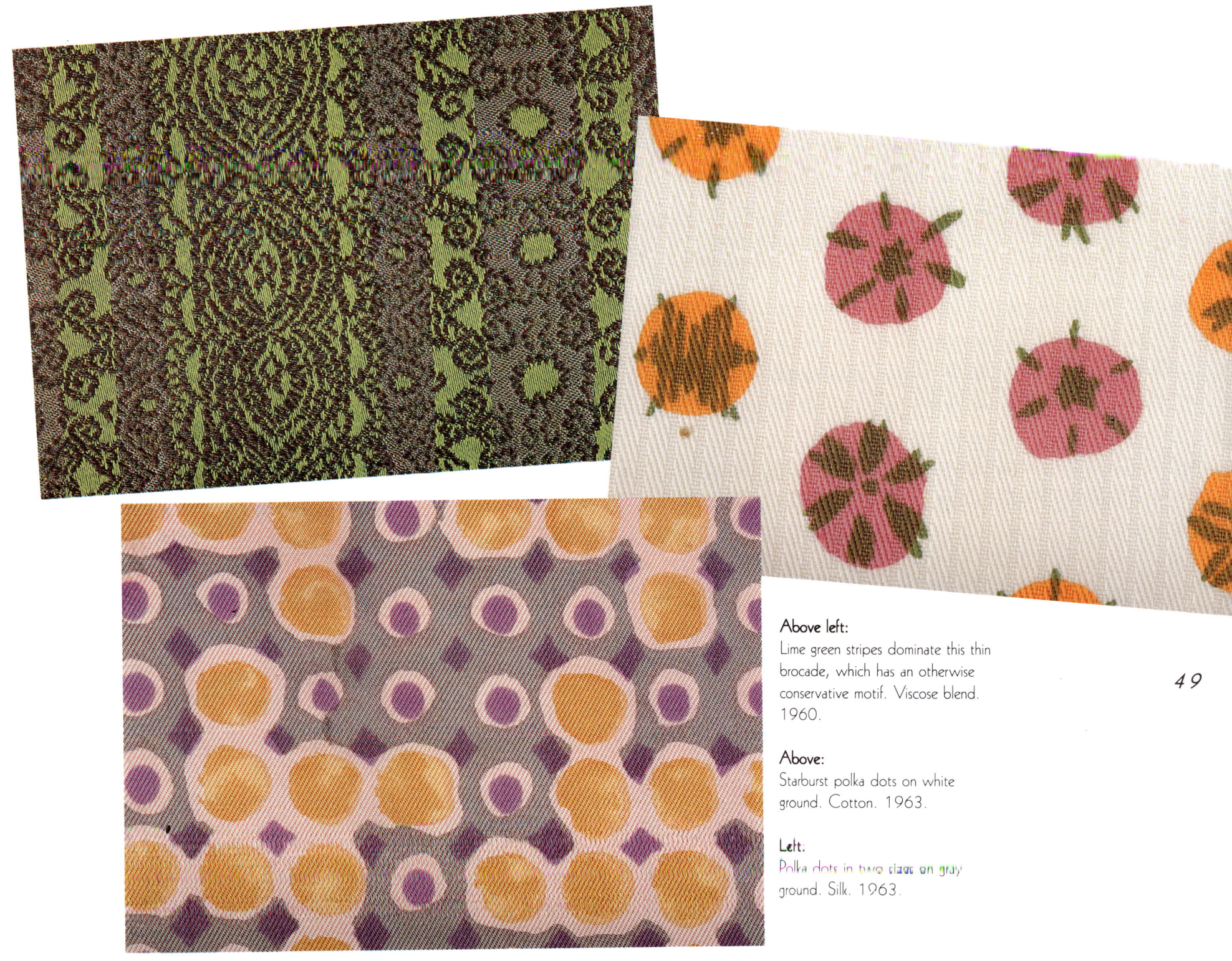

Above left:
Lime green stripes dominate this thin brocade, which has an otherwise conservative motif. Viscose blend. 1960.

Above:
Starburst polka dots on white ground. Cotton. 1963.

Left:
Polka dots in two sizes on gray ground. Silk. 1963.

49

Brightly colored polka-dots with rough black outlines. Cotton/rayon. 1961.

Bleeding dot pattern on aqua green ground. Cotton. 1963.

Packed design in blue, greens, and golds. Cotton. 1963.

Above:
White lines on olive-green ground.
Cotton/rayon blend twill. 1961.

Above right:
Stripes of hourglass shapes in hot colors
prescient of future. Silk. 1963.

Right:
Circle-filled squares irregularly aligned on
bone-white ground. Rayon twill. 1961.

Bold orange contrasts with olive, black, and white in geometric patchwork. Rayon. 1963.

Squares with overlaid shadow stripe in lighter shade. Cotton crêpe. 1963.

Geometric shapes in light blue and lavender on green ground. Silk. 1963.

Opposite:
Blocks of color form painterly, abstract plaid. Silk/polyester. 1961.

Watercolor patchwork. Rayon. 1961.

Four-tone, water-colored blue ovals on white ground. Cotton. 1963.

Small and large circles are strung together in stripes, with bold black outlines. Rayon/polyester blend. 1961.

56

Circles act as portholes on dark, mottled green and black ground. Polyester. 1963.

Blue rectangles on orange ground. Silk. 1963.

Short oblong stripes line up on yellow ground. Cotton. 1963.

Above:
Abstract shapes with outlines that create an impression of movement. Cotton. 1960.

Top left:
Double ring pattern on cranberry ground. Cotton blend. 1961.

Left:
Geometric design on white. Cotton novelty weave. 1960.

Right:
Abstract tribal design.
Cotton. 1960.

Below:
Abstract geometric design in stained-glass style.
Cotton. 1960.

Pink and green, four-point stars on white.
Cotton novelty weave. 1960.

Above:
Dark-plum polka-dot pattern with stylized flowers and linking stripes. Rayon. 1961.

Right:
Overlapping circles and explosive white spots. Cotton. 1960.

Above left:
Abstract roses on plum and black ground. Rayon blend. 1960.

Above:
Watercolor blocks of black and browns on white ground. Silk. 1961.

Left:
Painted circles form irregular, bleeding polka-dot pattern. Cotton. 1963.

Distinct, geometric pattern in Delft blue and gold. Cotton. 1961.

Above:
Brilliant colors in outlined geometric forms form snowflake motif on bird's-eye weave. Cotton. 1960.

Left:
X's and O's in bold patchwork. Polished cotton. 1963.

Opposite:
Geometric patterns on dry-brushed, black and gold ground. Cotton. 1961.

Abstracts

Above:
Abstract brown and green foliage on white ground. Cotton/polyester knit. 1961.

Left:
Abstract green and black shapes on white ground. Rayon blend. 1961.

Abstract, painterly design. Rayon/polyester. 1961.

Green "log piles" on white ground. Cotton/rayon. 1963.

Brown, green, and gold on cotton velvet. 1960.

Brown and black on white ground. Nylon. 1960.

Dotted, abstract design evokes image of lush foliage. Cotton. 1960.

Right:
Bright green light peeps through abstract crosshatching. Linen blend. 1961.

Below:
Abstract in browns, gold, and gray. Cotton. 1960

Random crosshatching with green accents. Cotton/polyester. 1963.

Left:
Watercolor lines and spots create an overall plaid effect. Rayon/polyester blend. 1961.

Below:
Sunburst polka-dot pattern. Rayon. 1961.

Above:
Abstract, vertical design in browns, green, and red. Rayon. 1960.

Above right:
Waterspot design in earth tones. Cotton/viscose blend. 1961.

Right:
Swirling brushstrokes of gray, cranberry, and mint on white ground. Nylon. 1960.

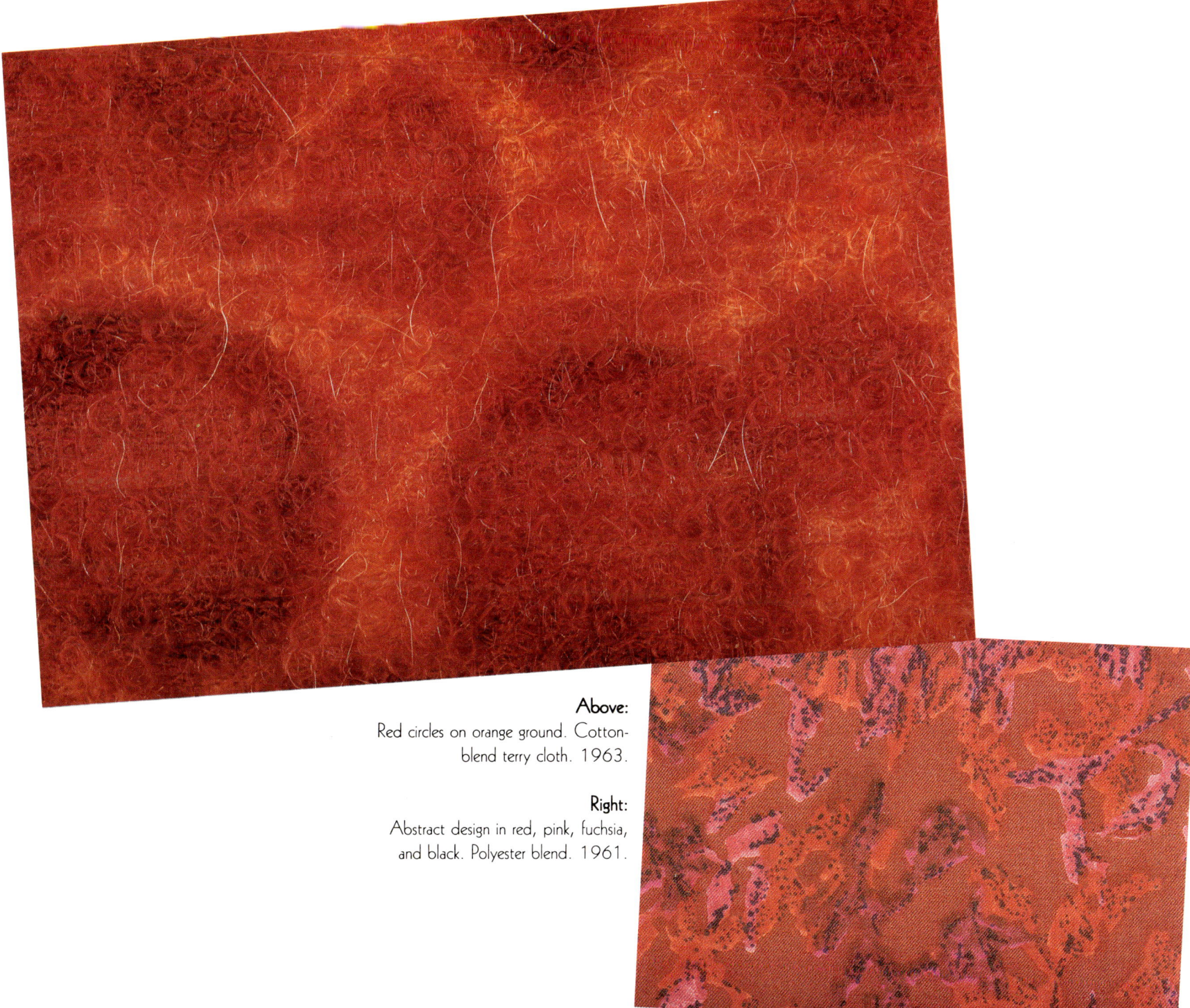

Above:
Red circles on orange ground. Cotton-blend terry cloth. 1963.

Right:
Abstract design in red, pink, fuchsia, and black. Polyester blend. 1961.

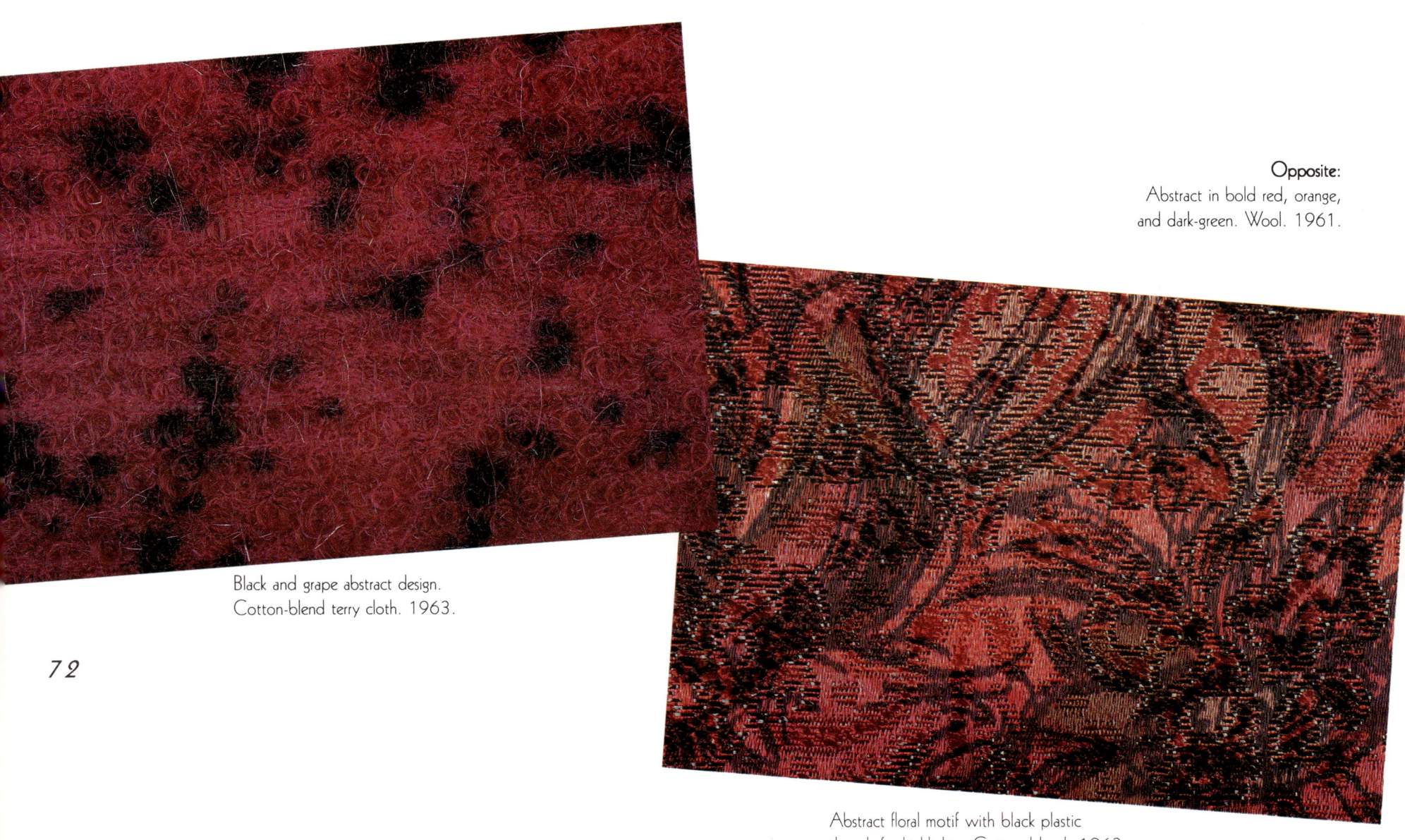

Black and grape abstract design. Cotton-blend terry cloth. 1963.

Opposite:
Abstract in bold red, orange, and dark-green. Wool. 1961.

Abstract floral motif with black plastic threads for highlights. Cotton blend. 1963.

Above left:
Abstract design in rust and grays. Cotton/polyester. 1961.

Above right:
Brushstrokes of bright ocean colors create a large, soft herringbone effect. Rayon. 1961.

Left:
Abstract watercolor design. Rayon. 1961.

75

Above:
Watercolor in blue and green tones on white ground. Rayon blend. 1961.

Left:
Abstract design in royal blue on white ground. Rayon. 1961.

Left:
Abstract blue, white, and lavender design. Cotton. 1960.

Below:
Blue watercolor with white floral accents. Nylon. 1960.

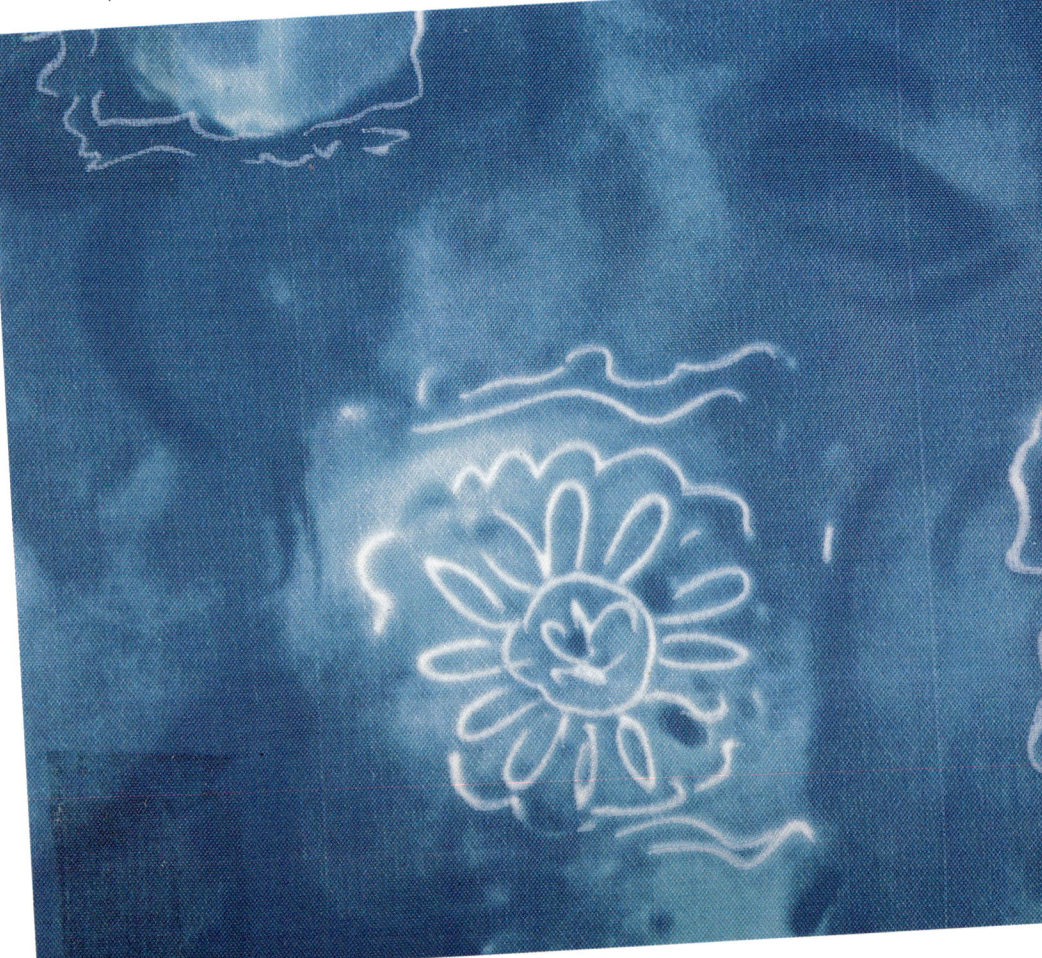

Abstract stripes on satin. Silk. 1961.

Pink watercolor design. Cotton blend twill. 1963.

Green-on-green, floral motif pattern. Silk. 1963.

The artist called this a "modern interpretation of knot work." Cotton blend. 1963.

Seemingly random concentrations of color on white ground. Cotton. 1960.

Above left:
Bright abstract. Cotton/rayon blend. 1963.

Above right:
Highly abstract flowers. Silk. 1963.

Left:
Abstract teepee shapes. Cotton. 1960.

Black and White

Blocks of black and erratic white lines form two-tone check pattern. Rayon. 1961.

Left: Black spots with shadow outline. Silk twill. 1963.

Below: Black spots on white ground. Corded rayon. 1963.

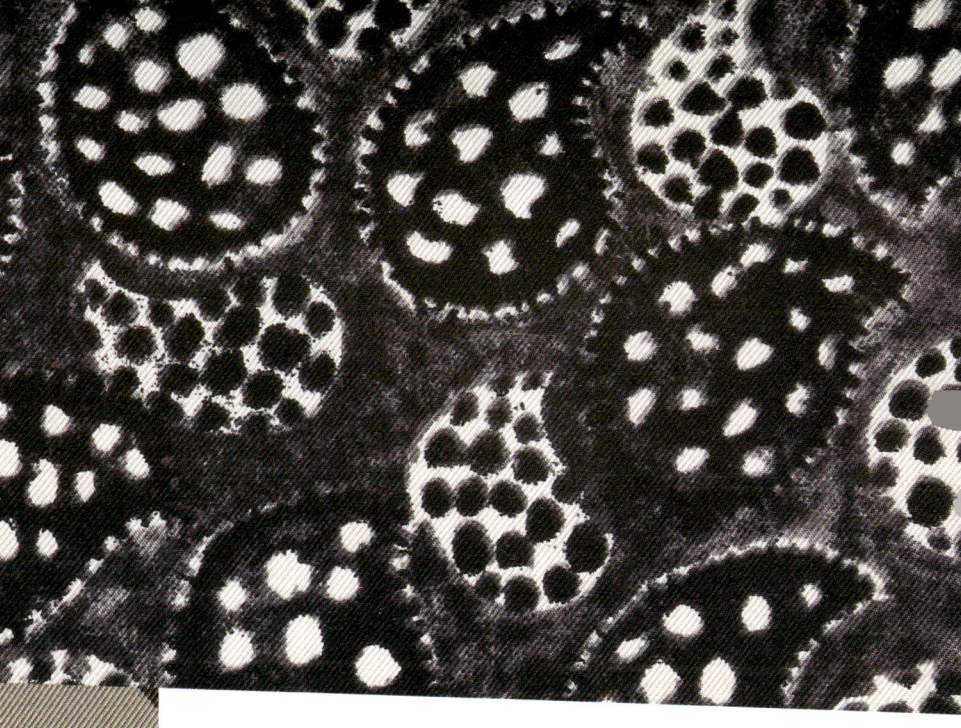

Above left:
Novelty weave imitates net-stocking knit. Cotton. 1960.

Above:
Modern paisley. Polyester blend. 1961.

Left:
Abstract, water lily design in greens on white. Silk. 1961.

Minimal use of black and gray creates cityscape on sand ground. 1961.

Above left:
Abstract landscape. Polyester-blend twill. 1961.

Above right:
Brushstrokes and splashes of color create an overall stormy night scene. Polyester blend. 1961.

Left:
Abstract, swirled design. Cotton. 1960.

Irregular dots in black and white. Polyester blend. 1963.

Tufts of black line up on pale gray ground. Rayon. 1963.

Abstract floral design. Cotton/rayon. 1961.

Flowers create highlights in gray, grid pattern. Rayon. 1961.

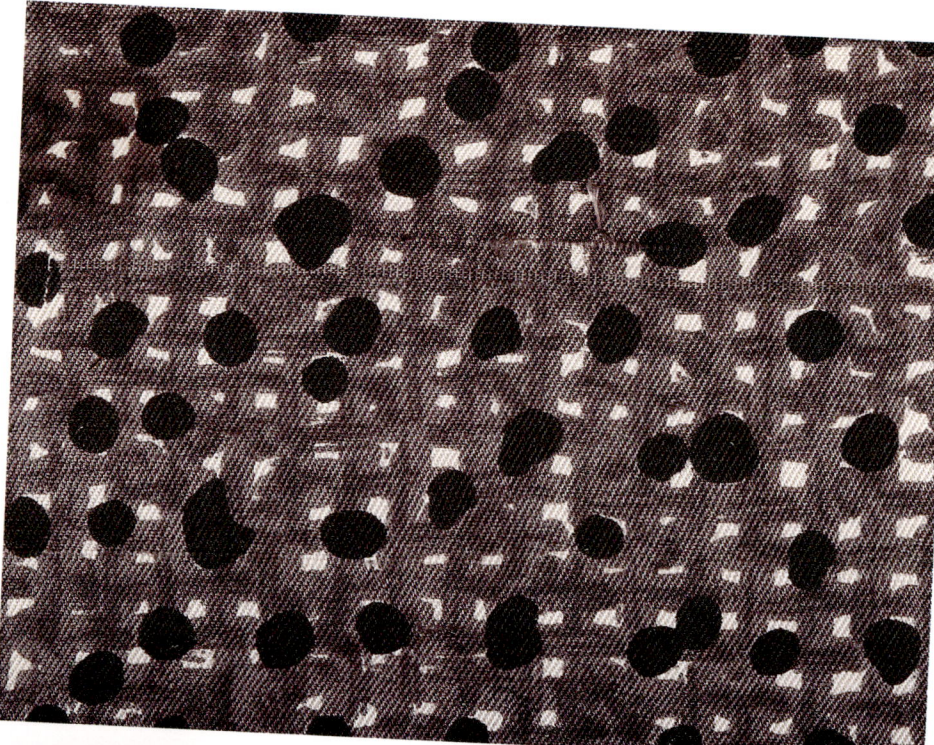

Above left:
Abstract plaid. Rayon twill. 1961.

Above right:
Charcoal grid with black dots, white ground. Silk. 1963.

Left:
Abstract design. Polyester blend. 1963.

Right:
Oriental orchard motif. Polyester blend. 1960.

Below:
Imitation of Asian script. Silk. 1963.

Novelty

Above:
Chinese pagoda and fisherman in garden scene. Rayon blend twill. 1961.

Above right:
Royal blue foliage on white background. Cotton. 1960.

Right:
Purple feather design on slate ground. Nylon blend. 1961.

Fruits on pink ground. Cotton. 1963.

Diagonal strokes create impression of lemons and limes. Cotton. 1960.

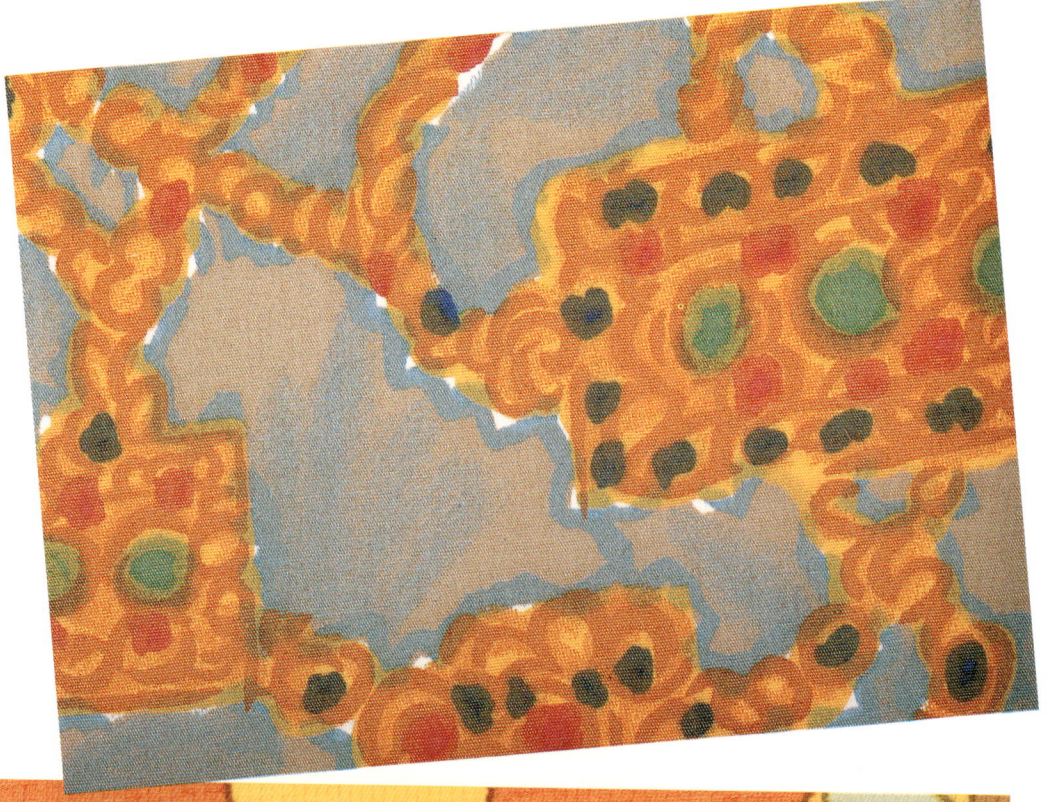

Above:
Abstract foliage. Cotton. 1963.

Above right:
Jewelry motif on watercolor ground. Cotton. 1963.

Right:
Bold floral motif. Cotton blend. 1960.

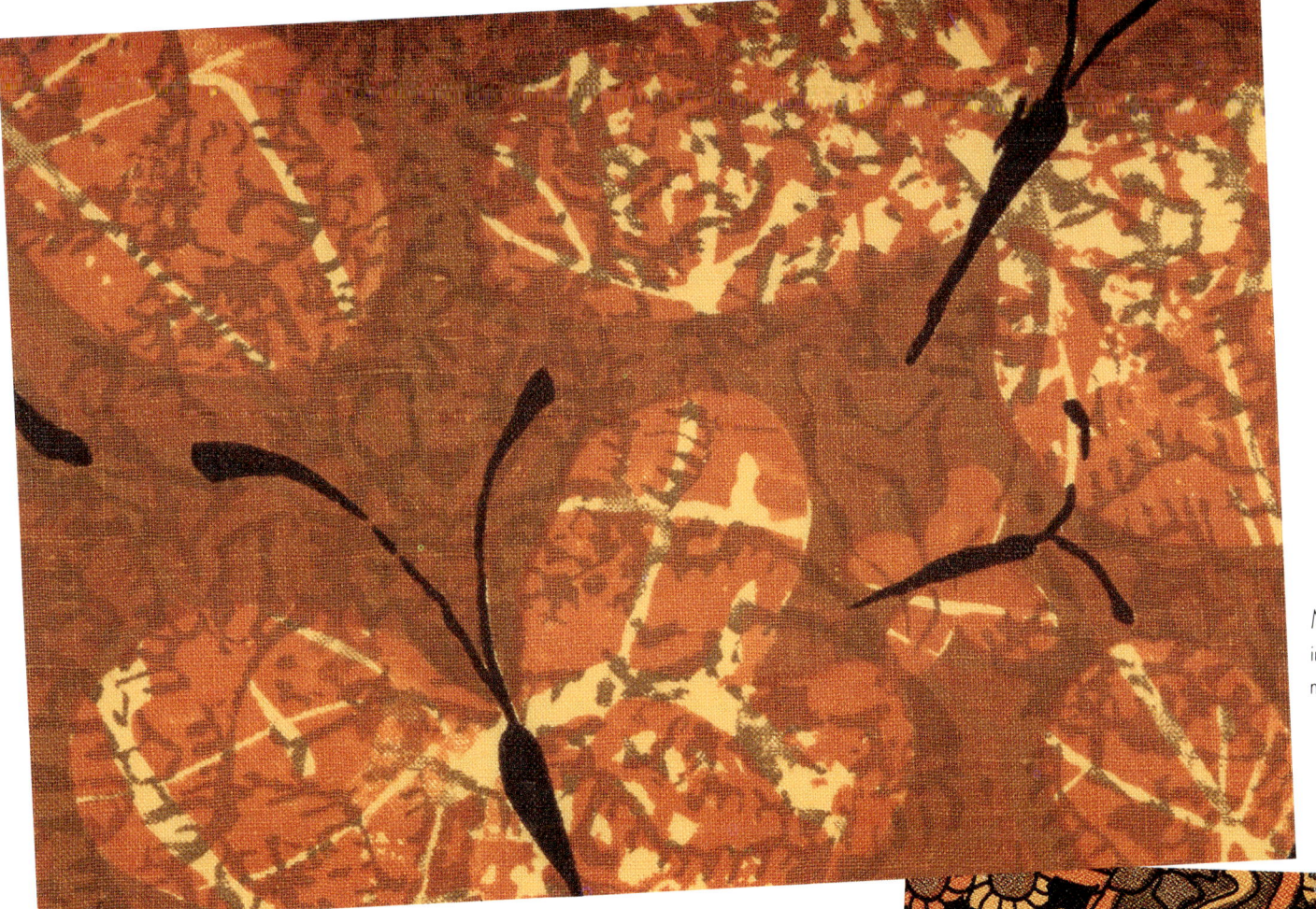

Mottled butterfly print imitates primitive batik dyeing methods. Cotton. 1960.

Butterflies and flowers on black ground. Rayon. 1963.

Left:
Sepia-tone photo print of almonds creates pocked and pitted texture. Cotton/rayon. 1961.

Below left:
Poppy photo print. Cotton. 1960.

Below:
Realistic chestnuts tumble across gray-white ground. Rayon. 1961.

Above:
Mixed-media pattern. Polished cotton. 1963.

Left:
Exotic colors in geometric form, with black, imitation stitching. Cotton/rayon. 1963.

Above:
Gem and setting motif in browns and grays. Cotton/polyester blend. 1961.

Right:
Mottled color and black, flower outlines form a background for abstract diamond motif. Cotton/polyester. 1961.

Drapery effect is created by swirling watercolor brushstrokes over white ground. Cotton. 1961.

Abstract in red and charcoal on white. Silk. 1963.

Painted lines imitate macramé. Silk/polyester. 1961.

Above left:
Abstract geometric/floral motif on plaid, blue-and-green ground. Cotton. 1963.

Above right:
Abstract fleur-de-lis. Polyester knit. 1961.

Left:
Abstract design. Rayon. 1963.

Upholstery and Home-decorating Fabrics

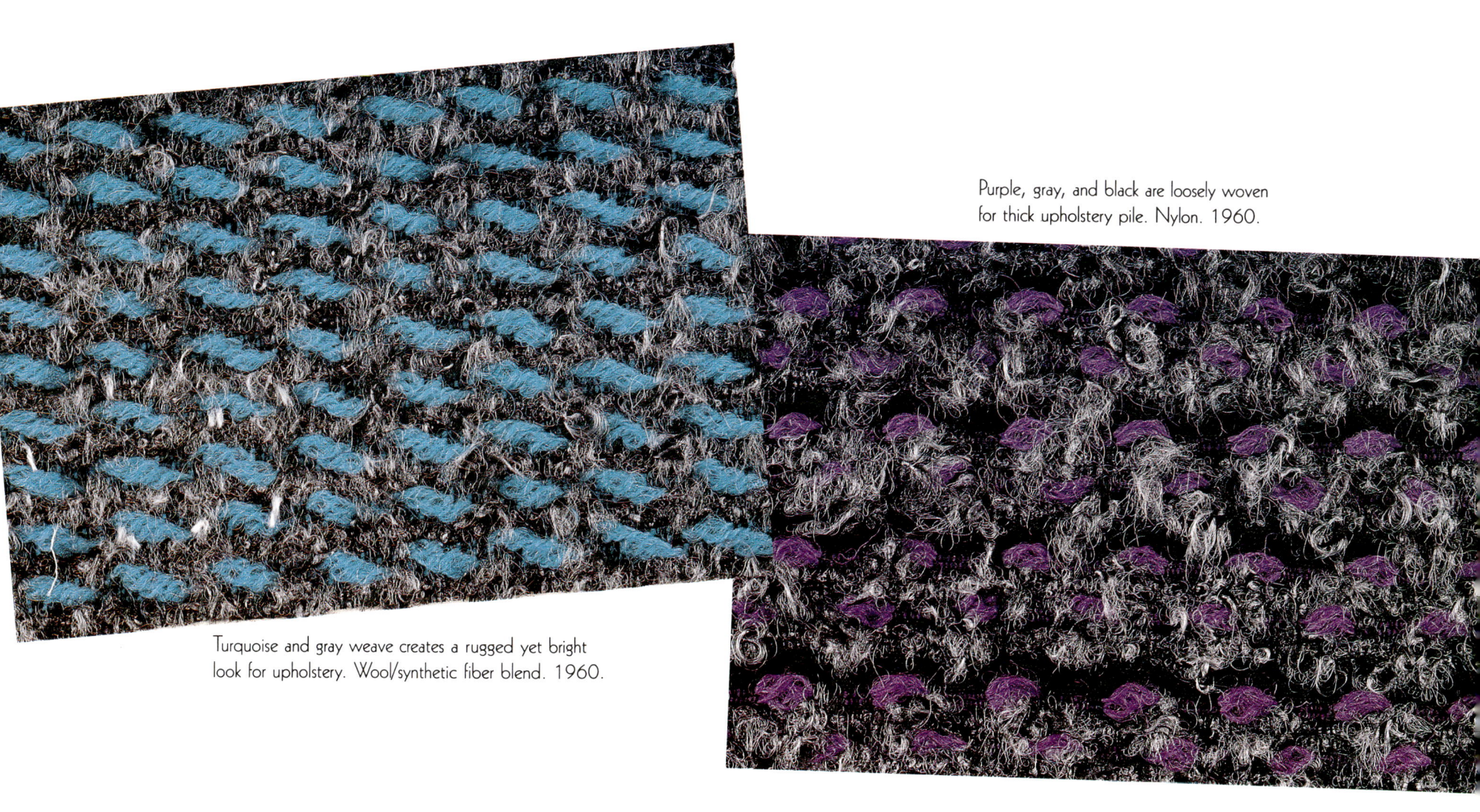

Purple, gray, and black are loosely woven for thick upholstery pile. Nylon. 1960.

Turquoise and gray weave creates a rugged yet bright look for upholstery. Wool/synthetic fiber blend. 1960.

Abstract plaid is created using metallic and rayon for strong, upholstery fabric. 1960.

The same pattern made more apparent by blending two browns and allowing the light blue cross stripes to stand in contrast.

Circular, black swirls on green satin ground. 1960.

Above:
Non-directional, abstract foliage on sea-blue ground creates underwater feel for this light-weight drapery or upholstery fabric. Silk. 1960.

Left:
Satin upholstery fabric with intensifying stripes of dots. Viscose blend. 1960.

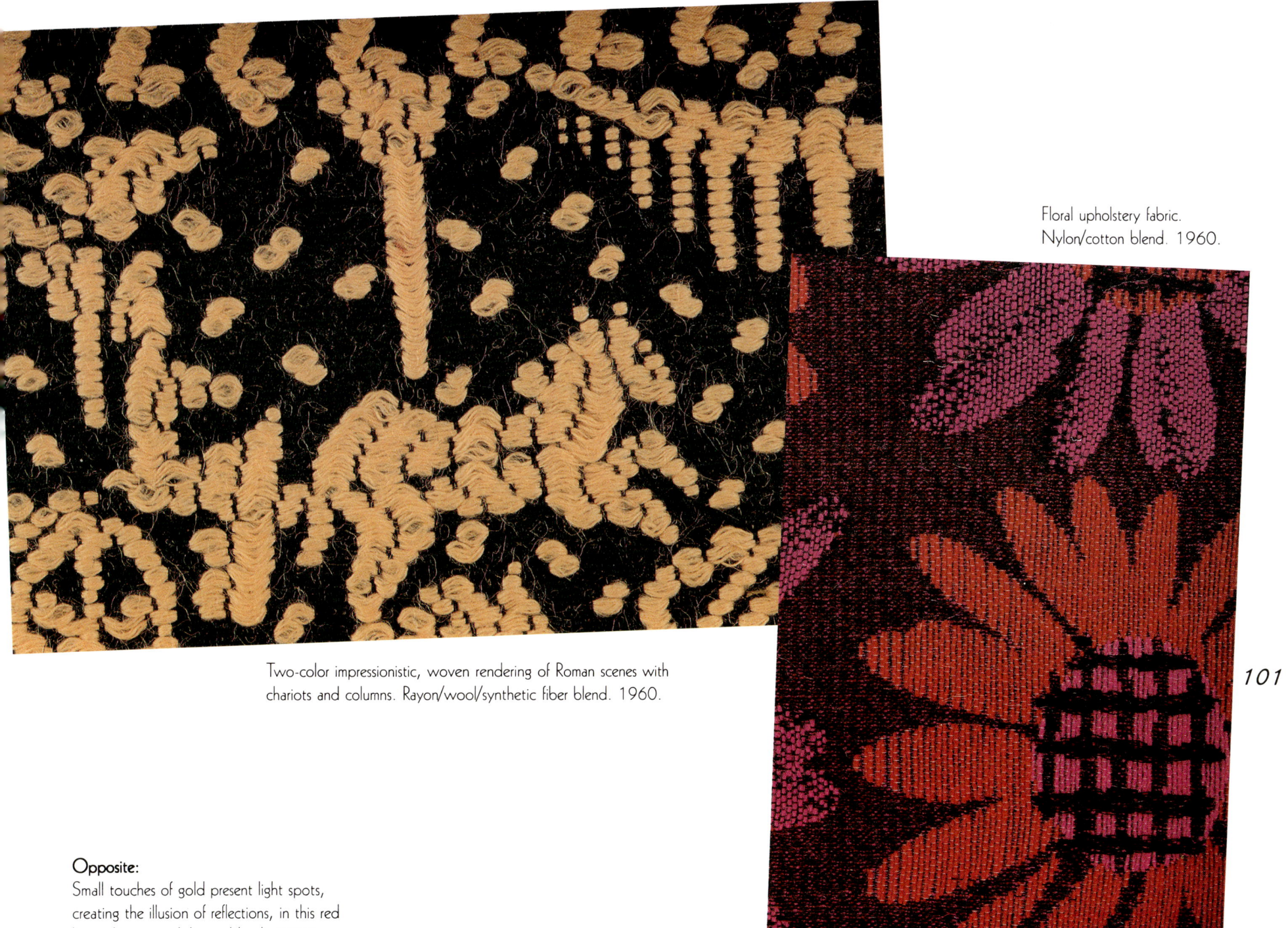

Two-color impressionistic, woven rendering of Roman scenes with chariots and columns. Rayon/wool/synthetic fiber blend. 1960.

Floral upholstery fabric. Nylon/cotton blend. 1960.

Opposite:
Small touches of gold present light spots, creating the illusion of reflections, in this red brocade weave. Viscose blend. 1960.

Above left:
Incredibly soft upholstery fabric with wintry plaid design. Viscose/wool/cotton. 1960.

Above right:
Magenta accents a mottled black and gray plaid upholstery weave. 1960.

Left:
Thick, felt-textured plaid pattern is raised above satin black cross stripes. 1960.

Above Left:
Golden hound's-tooth pattern makes a bold upholstery fabric statement. 1960.

Above right:
Abstract plaid of black on beige. 1960.

Left:
Loose interpretation of a plaid in sturdy upholstery weave. Viscose/silk. 1960.

White woven crewel work forms floral motif on blue and black brocade. 1960.

104

Bright basketweave over dark ground creates fetching upholstery pattern. Cotton/synthetic fiber blend. 1960.

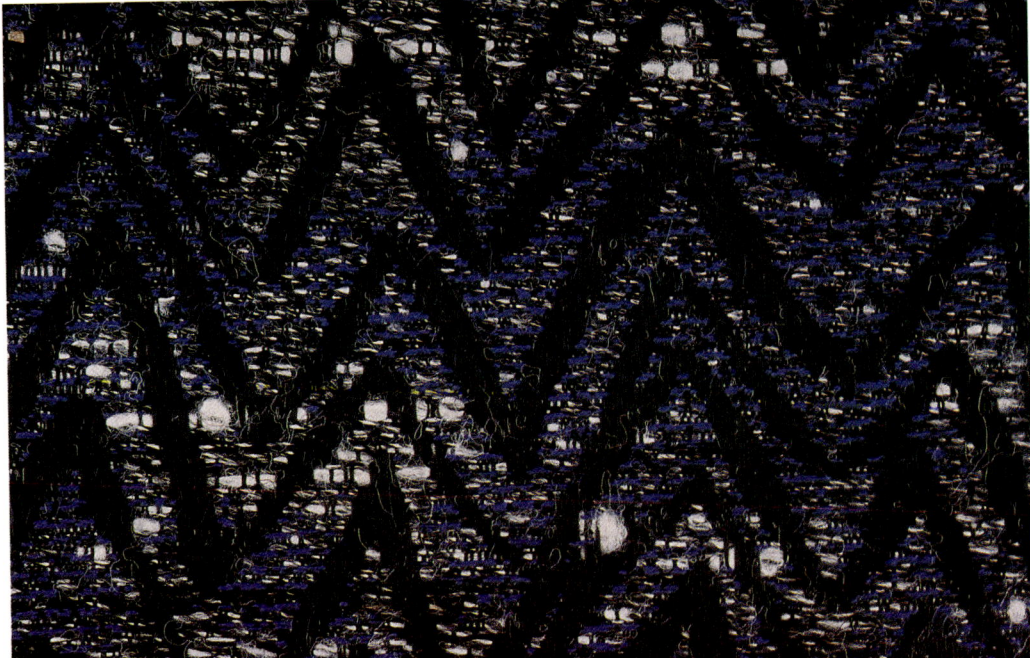

Black zigzag pattern is almost lost on mixed ground of this sturdy upholstery fabric. Wool blend. 1960.

Black and pink floral motif. 1960.

All-over floral motif on heavy upholstery weave, in light green and metallics on earth-tone ground. 1960.

Metallic roses on green ground. 1960.

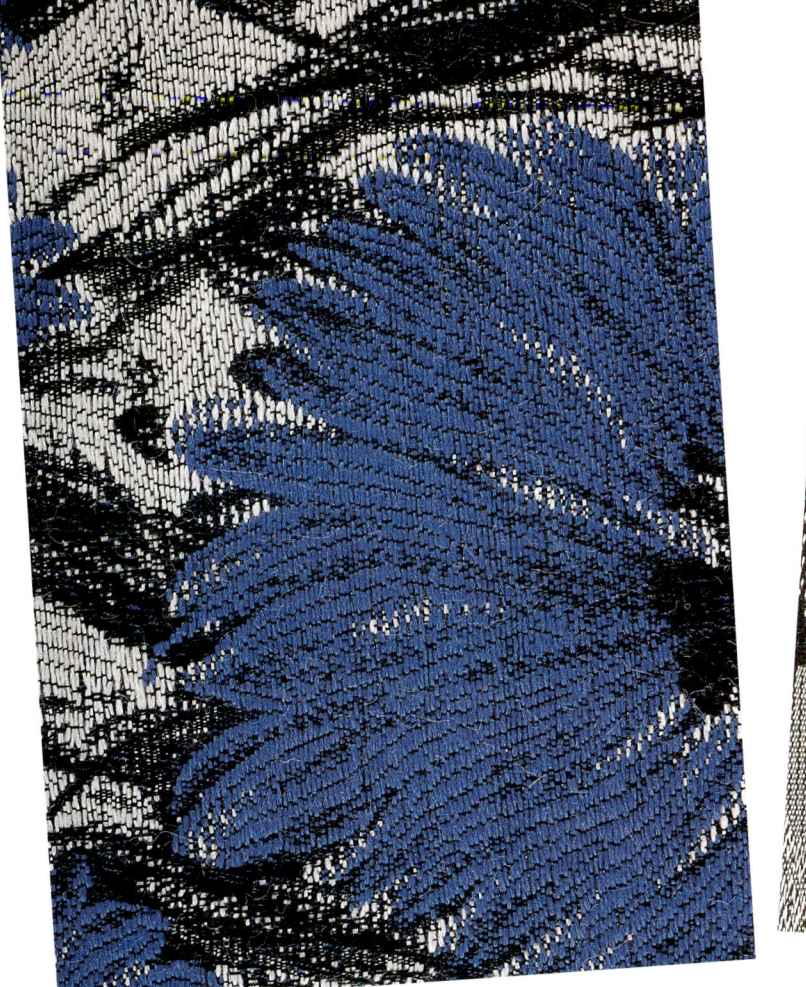

Soft lines give floral motif an impressionistic flair. Wool blend. 1960.

Black roses adorn gray and white, woven harlequin design. Wool/cotton blend. 1960.

Soft black floral pattern rises above metallic ground in upholstery fabric. 1960.

Above left:
Metallic and light blue floral motif imitates Chinese needlepoint on silk. 1960.

Above right:
Clover is scattered over a large, plaid framework in this upholstery fabric. 1960.

Left:
Floral crewel work and metallic crosshatching on neutral, satin ground. Viscose/cotton/plastic blend. 1960.

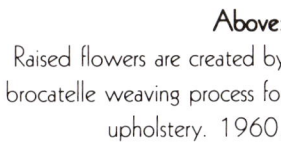

Above:
Raised flowers are created by brocatelle weaving process for upholstery. 1960.

Right:
Metallic-colored plastic fibers are used to decorate jewel-theme upholstery design. 1960.

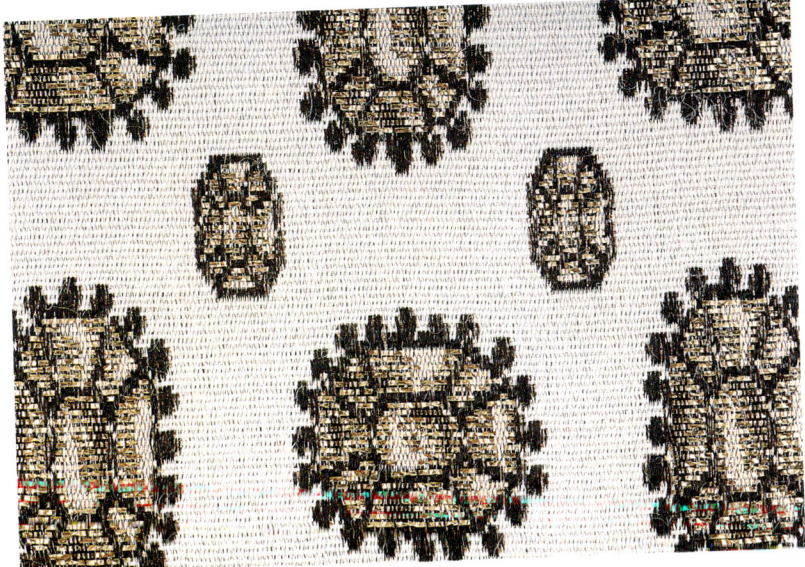

Floral motif for upholstery. Cotton/metallic plastic blend. 1960.

Metallic-colored plastic fibers decorate abstract floral stripes. 1960.

Rich, velvety appearance is created with raised design on black satin. 1960.

Abstract floral motif outlined with colored, metallic threads, for upholstery. 1960.

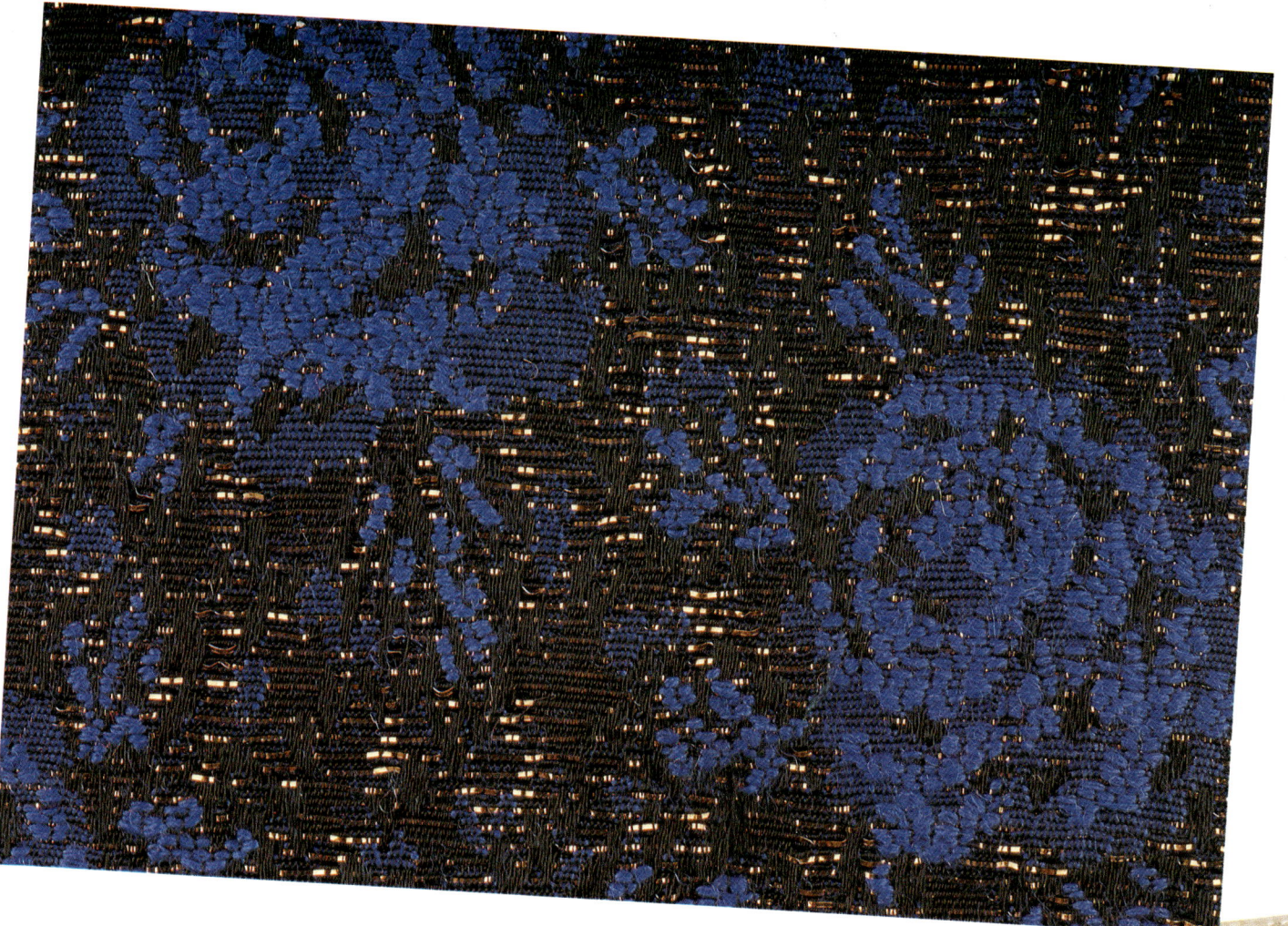

Above:
Blue roses are almost overshadowed by copper-colored, metallic threads in ground. Viscose/wool/metallic plastic blend. 1960.

Right:
Manmade fibers are used to create contrast between soft and sparkling, with subtle plaid pattern resulting. Viscose/wool blend. 1960.

Metallic and crimson fibers create stark contrast on black plaid. 1960.

Bibliography

Jerde, Judith, *Encyclopedia of Textiles*. New York: Facts On File, Inc., 1992.

Meller, Susan, and Joost Elffers, *Textile Designs*. New York: Harry N. Abrams, Inc., 1991.

Sears catalogs, 1959-1963.

Shih, Joy, *Couture Fabrics of the 50s*. Atglen, Pennsylvania: Schiffer Publishing, Inc., 1997.